Sing Alleluia!

Daphna Flegal

Illustrated by Suzanne Snyder

ISBN 0-687-05369-2

Manufactured in Hong Kong

98 99 00 01 02 03 04 05 06 07 – 10 9 8 7 6 5 4 3 2 1

Abingdon Press
Nashville

Look!

See the baby asleep on the hay.
Jesus, God's Son, is born this glad day.

Sing alleluia;
sing, sing, sing.
Sing alleluia
   to the baby King.

Listen!

The baby Jesus grew and grew.
He learned about God just like you do.

Sing alleluia;
sing, sing, sing.
Sing alleluia
   to the growing king.

Come!

The young boy is now a man.
He welcomes the children with
  a loving hand.

Sing alleluia;
sing, sing, sing.
Sing alleluia
  to the loving King.

Sit!

He teaches God's love to all
If we will stop and listen to his call.

Sing alleluia;
sing, sing, sing.
Sing alleluia
   to the teaching King.

Shout!

Here comes Jesus, God's peace to bring.
Hosanna! Hosanna! Let our praises ring.

Sing alleluia;
sing, sing, sing.
Sing alleluia
   to the peaceful King.

02853

Stop!

God's house is not a place to sell;
It's a place for God's love to dwell.

Sing alleluia;
sing, sing, sing.
Sing alleluia
   to the faithful King.

Remember!

Drink from the cup and eat
  the bread.
"Remember I love you,"
  Jesus said.

Sing alleluia;
sing, sing, sing.
Sing alleluia
  to the loving King.

Watch!

Here in the garden Jesus prays
For God to help him through these next days.

Sing alleluia;
sing, sing, sing.
Sing alleluia
   to the praying King.

Hide!

The soldiers have taken Jesus, our friend.
Peter will follow to see where it ends.

Sing alleluia?
How can we sing?
We're sad and afraid
   for Jesus, our King.

Crow!

"I do not know him,"
   says Peter with fear;
The rooster starts crowing
   as morning comes near.

Weep!
A cross on the hillside reminds us, each one,
That our friend Jesus was truly God's Son.

Sing!

The women are happy;
  they are surprised
To find the tomb empty:
  Jesus is alive!

Sing alleluia;
sing, sing, sing.
Sing alleluia
  to the RISEN KING!